Careers For Sports Fans

Interviews by Andrew Kaplan

Photographs by Eddie Keating and Carrie Boretz

CHOICES
The Millbrook Press
Brookfield, Connecticut

Produced in association with Agincourt Press.

Photographs by Edward Keating, except: Anne Henricksson
(Carrie Boretz), Andy MacPhail (Mark Bertram), Diane Olin
(David B. Sutton), Buck O'Neil (Debbie Douglas Sauer), Brenda
Paul (Carrie Boretz).

Cataloging-in-Publication Data

Kaplan, Andrew.
Careers for sports fans/interviews by Andrew Kaplan,
photographs by Edward Keating and Carrie Boretz.

64 p.; ill.: (Choices)
Bibliography: p.
Includes index.

Summary: Interviews with fourteen people who work in careers of
interest to young people who like school and professional sports.
1. Athletics.   2. Professional sports.   3. Physical education.
4. Coaching (Athletics).
I. Keating, Edward, ill.   II. Boretz, Carrie, ill.
III. Title.   IV. Series.
            1991   796 KAP
ISBN 1-56294-023-6

Contents

Introduction

In this book, 14 people who work in sports-related fields talk about their careers — what their work involves, how they got started, and what they like (and dislike) about it. They tell you things you should know before beginning a sports-related career, and show you how being a sports fan can lead to many different types of jobs.

Many sports-related jobs are found in the major professional spectator sports such as baseball, football, basketball, and hockey. But just as many can be found in such associated areas as the media (sportswriter, sports announcer) and the business of sports (sports lawyer, sports product manager). You don't have to play sports to have a sports-related career. To work at the National Baseball Hall of Fame, for instance, you only have to like baseball.

The 14 careers described here are just the beginning, so don't limit your sights. At the end of this book, you'll find short descriptions of a dozen more careers you may want to explore, as well as suggestions on how to get more information. There are many business opportunities in the world of professional athletics. If you're a sports fan, you'll find a wide range of career choices open to you.

Joan B. Storey, M.B.A., M.S.W.
Series Career Consultant

"I'm paid to be somewhere
that I'd be anyway."

PETE ARBOGAST
SPORTS ANNOUNCER
Los Angeles, California

WHAT I DO:
I have two jobs, both of which involve sports. My main job is doing sportscasting and sports news spots for radio station KNX in Los Angeles. My other job is with the Los Angeles Dodgers doing public address announcing for all of their home games.

At KNX, I cover a wide variety of sports. I'm the football and basketball voice of the University of Southern California Trojans. I also cover the L.A. Lakers basketball team and the L.A. Kings hockey team, and no matter what season it is, I do sports news — two minutes every half-hour for a four-hour shift every afternoon. To prepare these spots, I come to the station, check the wire services, and call the local teams to see what's happening.

Pete covers a variety of sports on his radio show.

For the Dodgers, I announce eighty-one regular season games and two preseason games each year. My routine is pretty consistent. I get to the stadium about an hour before the game. I grab a bite to eat and read a few pregame announcements about programs and tickets for sale. Then I announce the game, which takes two to three hours. Unlike radio work, public address announcing has no commentary or opinions. I just tell the fans in the stadium what's happening — who's coming to bat, who's coming up, who's on the mound.

HOW I GOT STARTED:
Although I've always liked going to games, I really believe there's something special about listening to them. When I was 9 or 10, I used to drive my friends crazy. We'd be running up and down the basketball court,

and I'd be announcing the plays as we were making them. My friends would tell me to shut up and play.

But I never did — I just kept announcing. My high school had a radio station and I announced football games. I also kept in practice by announcing games into a tape recorder. Later, at college, I studied radio broadcasting and broadcast journalism.

After college, I had a series of jobs in small towns. My first job was in Twin Falls, Idaho. I did everything — news, sports, commercials, and overnight work. Then I moved to a little desert town called Victorville, California,

and then on to Porterville in central California. Porterville was a good place for me because it had a lot of sports — high school, college, and minor league baseball.

While I was in Porterville, I got a great opportunity. I was listening to a sports talk show, and the guy was pleading with people to call in, but everybody was watching the Dodgers' playoff game instead. Finally, he said that if some people called in, he'd let them do some play-by-play of the game over the air. I called in and announced the bottom half of the ninth inning. A guy from a large station in Riverside, California, heard me and offered

Pete makes some pregame announcements.

Pete calls a home game at Dodger Stadium.

me a job doing news and sports. About a year later, I got back to Los Angeles.

HOW I FEEL ABOUT IT:
Both these jobs are dream jobs for me. My work allows me to follow the teams I love. It's amazing. I'm paid to be somewhere that I'd be anyway. And while I'm at the games, I'm entertaining people and informing them. People listen to my broadcasts, learn a little, and in the end say, "That was fun to listen to."

WHAT YOU SHOULD KNOW:
If you want to be a play-by-play announcer, take a tape recorder and go to every sports event you can. Call the game into the machine, then go home and listen to it. Pick out what you like and what

you don't like. Stop doing the things you don't like and try some new stuff the next time. When you finally get a tape you're comfortable with, ask a local announcer to listen to it. Listen to the criticism, and practice, practice, practice. Also, it's absolutely necessary to listen to other broadcasters so you can learn something about broadcasting style.

When you get to the upper echelons in radio, the pay can be pretty good. Last year, between KNX and the Dodger announcing, I made about $65,000. If I were doing radio play-by-play for the Dodgers, I would probably make two or three times that amount. Television salaries are even higher. For both radio and TV, however, pay depends a lot on the sport and the city.

"I've been to Australia,
Japan, Africa, and all over
Europe."

ANNE HENRICKSSON

PRO TENNIS PLAYER

Mill Valley, California

WHAT I DO:
I'm a professional tennis player, and I play in about twenty or so tournaments each year. Most players play in sixteen or seventeen tournaments a year, but I've always played in more because I like playing tennis. When I'm not on the road playing in tournaments, I'm at home in California practicing.

For the past ten years, my routine has been pretty much the same — two to three weeks of practice followed by three or four weeks of tournaments. When I'm home, training, my schedule is pretty consistent. I play a couple of hours of tennis in the morning. Then I take a break, and in the afternoon I either play a few more hours or do some other kind of fitness training such as weight

Anne returns a volley during a match at the U.S. Open.

lifting. When I'm playing in a tournament, though, things are always different. When I go to a foreign country, I have to adapt to the time change. Also, it's not as easy to train. There are matches going on, and the facilities aren't available. So you have to do what you can — you have to adapt.

HOW I GOT STARTED:
I started playing tennis when I was about 11 and played in my first tournament when I was 12. I grew up in Minnesota, where it was very easy to win because there just weren't that many good tennis players around. The competition level wasn't high, but in a strange way this helped me because it gave me a lot of confidence. I'd beat everyone in Minnesota pretty easily. Then I'd play in a national tournament and get killed because the players were so good. But when I got back to

Anne practices her game several hours each day.

Minnesota, I always won and got an ego boost again.

After high school, I got an athletic scholarship to Arizona State University. But I had a problem with the coach there, so after a year I transferred to the University of California at Los Angeles. The tennis there was good, but the school was expensive and I didn't have a scholarship anymore. After two years at UCLA, I decided to turn pro to earn enough money to graduate. But I did better than I thought I would, so I kept on playing. I've been on the professional circuit ever since.

HOW I FEEL ABOUT IT:
I'm playing tennis, a game I love, and obviously that's great. But beyond that, what I like most is that I've been able to get something different out of it every year.

There's a lot of travel. I've already been to Australia, Japan, Singapore, Taiwan, Africa, and all over Europe. Next week, I'm going to Moscow. And there are still places I haven't been. Tennis continues to be satisfying for me because I'm always learning, both about the game and about the world.

Tennis life does have its drawbacks, however. With all the traveling and the hotel rooms, tennis can be a solitary, lonely existence. Sustaining relationships is very hard. For someone who's not in the tennis world, it's difficult to understand why you'll be away for four weeks, then back for a couple of weeks, and then away again. Long-distance relationships haven't worked for me, and don't work for a lot of women on the tour. Some married players take their husbands on the tour with them, usually as coaches or managers. It can work, but it's intense because they're with each other twenty-four hours a day.

WHAT YOU SHOULD KNOW: To start out, you need help. Because tennis demands a great deal of time and energy, you really can't do much else. Although I'd recommend trying it, it's tough to go to college and play at the same time. And while I've seen people split their time between tennis and other jobs, it almost never works. Once you're out of school, you need to give tennis your full attention. And that means, until you're successful, you have to have financial help. I make enough from tennis to support myself, but some people on the tour are sponsored by their families or friends. And some people, of course, make millions.

In the time I've been playing tennis, it's gone from a sport with a modest audience to a really big business. In some ways this is good — there's more money around, so more players can be supported by it. But there's also more greed, particularly among coaches and parents. Parents push their children much too hard, and that's bad for the kids' mental and physical health. It's much better when the kids are out there, doing their own thing, and pursuing tennis in their own ways.

A call is disputed during a doubles match.

"I'm the third generation of a baseball family."

ANDY MACPHAIL

BASEBALL EXECUTIVE

Minneapolis, Minnesota

WHAT I DO:

As general manager of the Minnesota Twins, I'm responsible for obtaining the players who will make up the team. I'm in charge of player development and scouting, as well as negotiating contracts and trades. What my job doesn't cover is the marketing side, which includes ticket sales, concessions, television contracts — that sort of thing.

My staff includes a director of scouting, who's responsible for player procurement; a director of minor leagues; a vice president of player personnel, who's the link between the major and minor league teams; and a director of baseball administration, who works on special projects such as our new spring training facility in Florida. From each of these people, I

Andy handles the Twins' administrative details.

get regular reports on players they think we should try to get, on our minor league prospects, and on players on other teams. I'm constantly analyzing this information, both to help us with the current season and to plan for the club's future.

What I do on a day-to-day basis depends on the time of the year. During the baseball season, my job consists mostly of reacting to circumstances as they come up. For example, if there's an injury that creates a hole on the team, I may have to make a trade or see who we can call up from one of our minor league teams.

In the fall, after the season is over, I prepare for baseball's winter meetings, where team executives gather to talk about changes in the game and to make trades. The rest of the winter is almost totally consumed by

Andy chats with a reporter before a home game.

contract negotiations. After we finish with that, there's spring training, when I work with the manager and the coaching staff to evaluate the players and try to figure out who's going to make the team and who's not.

HOW I GOT STARTED:
I'm the third generation of a baseball family. Over the years, my grandfather, Larry MacPhail, was president of three different teams. My father, Lee MacPhail, was also a general manager and president of the American League. From the time I was young, I knew that I would try working in baseball, to see whether I would like it as much as they did.

I got my first job in base-ball when I was just out of college. I went to work for the Chicago Cubs, as business manager for one of their minor league teams. After six years with the Cubs, I then went to work for the Houston Astros, who promoted me to assistant general manager. Finally, I came over to the Twins as vice president of player personnel, and I was later promoted to general manager.

HOW I FEEL ABOUT IT:
At this point, there isn't too much I would change about my job or the game. Baseball has always been popular, and more and more people seem to be enjoying it every day. Beyond that, no two seasons are alike. Even as you're react-

ing to one situation, something new usually crops up to change it. Everything keeps shifting from day to day and season to season. It may be a tough job, but at least it's never dull.

WHAT YOU SHOULD KNOW:
A large percentage of the people in baseball front-office work start out with some connection to the game. They're either from baseball families or have been players themselves. But that's changing. There are more people from the outside than there used to be.

The biggest obstacle to breaking into this type of work is the limited number of available jobs. With a management background, you could start in minor league work. But the higher you move, the fewer jobs there

are. There are only twenty-six major league teams, and each has only one general manager. So the competition for these jobs is pretty tough. There is turnover, however.

Although it's obviously not what the top players make, the pay is good enough. But the real problem is the lack of job security. Four or five general managers lose their jobs every year.

During the season, this is an around-the-clock job. When I'm in town, I work from 9:00 in the morning until 10:30 at night. The rest of the time I'm either on the road with the Twins or traveling around our minor league system. However, these hours are typical of most jobs that are rewarding and fun. And I don't think about the number of hours because I'm doing what I want to do.

Andy takes time out to watch batting practice.

"The biggest problem a new official has is how to gain respect."

JAY SHARRERS

HOCKEY OFFICIAL

Niagara Falls, Ontario

WHAT I DO:
I'm a linesman for the National Hockey League. To understand what I do, you first have to understand a little about hockey. In a game situation, there are three officials — the referee and two linesmen. The referee calls all the penalties and decides whether a goal has been scored. While the referee is watching the puck, the linesmen watch the lines to make sure that neither the players nor the puck goes offsides. Linesmen are also responsible for preventing or breaking up any fights between the players.

Work for me starts at the beginning of the exhibition schedule, which is around the middle of September, and lasts at least until the regular season ends in late March. The best officials keep work-ing until the playoffs end, which is usually in late May. In an average month, you're on the road anywhere from twelve to twenty days. It varies from month to month, depending on the schedule.

Although they have no home arenas, linesmen work on a somewhat regional basis. About 30 percent of the games we work are in a particular area. For example, most of the games I work are in the Buffalo-Toronto area. But I still do a lot of long-distance travel when I'm occasionally assigned to do games in Los Angeles and Vancouver. And referees travel even more. They almost never work back to back games in the same city.

HOW I GOT STARTED:
I played hockey until I was 15. After that, Hope, the little town where I grew up in British Columbia, didn't have much in the way of organized

As a linesman, Jay has to watch for offsides penalties.

hockey. Since I really loved the game, though, I got involved in refereeing instead.

I was working in the men's recreational league and for a local minor league team when I was noticed by some people who were recruiting officials for higher levels of hockey. Things progressed quickly from there. When I was 18, I moved to Vancouver and a year later, I became a linesman for the Western Hockey League, a junior hockey league in western Canada. I did that for four years. Then this past year, I was hired by the NHL.

HOW I FEEL ABOUT IT:

What I enjoy most about being a linesman is that I really look forward to going to work. There isn't any one thing that I can point to as being the best. I just really enjoy going to work. The biggest drawback, however, is the travel. This sometimes gets me down, and it isn't always conducive to a good social life. But no matter where I am, I still take pleasure in doing the job.

On the ice itself, the biggest problem for a new official like me is how to gain respect. You're in a new league, and most of the older players have never seen you. You have to work hard to gain the confidence of these players and their coaches.

Jay laces up his skates in the locker room before a game.

Without being too aggressive and too strong, I have to show that I deserve to be there. I have to be tough, and let them know that I won't be pushed around. But I also don't want to antagonize them unnecessarily or seem arbitrary.

WHAT YOU SHOULD KNOW:

There are certain basic requirements for becoming a linesman. Due to the speed of the game, you have to be a fast, confident skater. Also, like any other official in any sport, you have to be able to ignore comments from the players. You have to realize that they're just yelling at the striped shirt, not at you personally. If you do take it personally, you won't last. It will eat away at you and affect your performance.

Even after you're hired, there are still some hurdles to clear. Officials are ranked, and the rankings affect both working status and pay. If, over a period of years, you're consistently ranked in the bottom third of the league, that is just cause for termination of your contract. Also, a low rating will prevent you from earning more money. The higher your ranking, the more playoff games you'll work, and playoff games represent pay above your base salary.

Base pay depends on years of service. As a linesman trainee, I work half-time in the NHL and half-time in the American League. The NHL pays me $20,000. A full-time NHL linesman earns from $30,000 to $69,000. Playoffs can add up to another $15,000, depending on the number of rounds you work.

Only a skilled skater can keep up with the action.

"To do this job well, it's crucial to understand the subtleties of your client's sport."

KIM STRATOS
SPORTS LAWYER
Miami, Florida

WHAT I DO:

I'm a litigator and sports lawyer, with my sports practice consisting mainly of professional athletes. Being a litigator means that I try cases in court. For the athletes I represent, I primarily handle contract cases, but I'll also get involved with copyright issues, tax matters, and even house closings — any legal need that a client might have. For some players, I also function as a sports agent, in the sense that I negotiate contracts and product endorsements.

The work also has a less formal side, though, because most pro athletes are young, and unaccustomed to managing money. You have to help them with things like buying a house, planning for taxes, and making investments. Some agents have in-house

Kim looks over a client's endorsement contract.

people who provide investment services. Other agents, such as myself, refer the players to brokers and tax lawyers who are experts in their fields.

Although I function as both a sports agent and a sports lawyer, the titles are not interchangeable. Both can negotiate contracts, but that's where the similarity ends. If an athlete has an agent who is not a lawyer, he or she will still need a lawyer to look over the contracts and take care of other legal needs.

HOW I GOT STARTED:

I've known Rob Murphy, who plays for the Boston Red Sox, since we were in high school. When I became a lawyer, he was still in minor league ball but was just reaching the stage at which he was considering hiring an agent. I took over his negotiations, and stayed with him as he rose up the ladder. Through his referrals, I've been able to get other clients, mainly baseball players.

Things would never have worked out this well, however, if I hadn't been a sports fan myself. To do this job well, it's crucial to understand the subtleties of your client's sport. If you aren't familiar with the idiosyncrasies of the game, you can't negotiate well, no matter how good your legal skills are. For example, if you represent a relief pitcher, you need to understand the importance of a statistic such as the number of inherited runners — runners already on base when a pitcher enters the game — and why a win-loss record may not be a good measure of a player's performance. You also need to know about specific clubs, and the clauses they will or will not negotiate.

HOW I FEEL ABOUT IT:
If I had to choose a favorite part of the job, it would probably be contract negotiations because it's such an intellectual challenge, requiring analytic skills as well as a willingness to banter. When the club throws something that looks like a negative statistic at you, you have to be able to come right back at them with a reason why that statistic isn't what it seems to be.

The thing that I like least about this job is the babysitting. Because they've been stars their whole lives, some of these players are used to being pampered. Some play-

Studying fine print is a big part of Kim's job.

Kim discusses a contract with team management.

ers want their agents to take care of any problem they have, no matter what it is. There's one well-known story about an agent who was woken up by a call in the middle of the night from a client who had a problem with his plumbing. There was no hot water, and he wanted his agent to fix it.

WHAT YOU SHOULD KNOW:
If you want to get into sports law, there are several things to consider. You need to develop the basic legal skills required of any lawyer, but you also need to know both the game and the business of sports. It helps to go to meetings of groups like the Sports Lawyers' Association. There, you can learn about the business and the people who are in it.

What you earn depends on the clients you represent. In baseball, for example, there are two ways of billing fees, by commission and by an hourly rate. For a commission, the usual rate is 5 percent — that is, you get 5 percent of whatever your client makes on a deal that you negotiate. Some agents charge additional fees for financial services and get percentages of endorsement deals. Either way, billing by commission or by the hour, it's possible to make a lot of money in sports law. But many sports lawyers still practice other kinds of law because — as you'd discover if you looked up the agents for all the big-name, big-money athletes in professional sports — most are represented by just a few agents.

"What I like about this work
is that it changes every day."

RON BLUM

SPORTSWRITER

New York, New York

WHAT I DO:

I cover sports for The Associated Press. The AP is a news service with offices all over the world. The AP staff writes articles that are transmitted electronically to newspapers, which pay AP for the right to publish them. This way, local newspapers in small towns can report on national and world news.

Most reporters have "beats," or particular subjects they cover. My beat is the business of sports. Instead of writing previews of upcoming sports events or doing game stories, I spend most of my time writing about economic and legal issues in professional sports. This can include players' contract negotiations, union matters, salary arbitration, and lawsuits. Some of the bigger stories I've been involved

Ron looks up some facts for an article on baseball.

with have been the collusion cases, in which the baseball owners were found guilty of conspiring to keep players' salaries down; Pete Rose's gambling and tax cases; and the San Francisco earthquake that disrupted the 1989 World Series. I also write about the relationship between television and sports, especially the negotiations and the contracts between the networks and the leagues.

I get my ideas for articles from different places. Some articles are assigned to me; others come from daily contacts I make with sources in the field. If you talk to the right people, you eventually find out what's happening. Because I write mostly on baseball, I'm constantly in touch with the general managers of teams and player agents. This is especially true when there's an ongoing story, such as the baseball lockout of 1990 when the owners refused to open spring training camps. At one point, I spent seventy-three consecutive days covering the story without a day off.

HOW I GOT STARTED:

I always was a baseball fan. Later, I developed an interest in writing. I wrote about sports for my high school and college newspapers, and so it was natural for me to keep writing about sports after college.

Right after I graduated, I got a job with a computer company working on a sports information data base. There, I was responsible for organizing and recording statistics on different sports. After that, I came over to the AP, where I've been for almost five years.

HOW I FEEL ABOUT IT:

What I like about this work is that it changes every day. There is no routine. Every story is a different situation. Even when you deal with the same people, the circumstances keep changing. One day George Steinbrenner is running the Yankees and the next day he's not, so you never know what to expect or what you're going to hear. It's not like some jobs, where you're constantly doing the same thing over and over again.

WHAT YOU SHOULD KNOW:

It's a tough job because you often need to talk to people who don't want to talk to you.

Ron hurries to finish a story before the deadline.

Ron reviews an article with a colleague.

You also need to accept that, because of daily newspaper deadlines, you're going to have to unravel and write about a whole mess of material in what usually seems like no time at all. Once you get comfortable with the breakneck pace and learn not to panic, however, you can analyze the situation, get down to work, and write your story.

To get into this work, you've got to hone your writing skills and be aggressive. You've got to write as much as you can, write as succinctly as you can, and write quickly. On top of that, you have to become known. You can start by doing part-time work at a local paper or a college press box, making contacts with other sports-writers, and getting to know the athletes and the coaches.

The hours are whatever the story demands. Some weeks are normal; at other times 100-hour weeks pop out of nowhere. There's also travel for important events like the All-Star Game, the World Series, soccer's World Cup — which I also cover — and so on. Even though the AP is large and has offices all over the world, New York reporters still travel to these types of events.

The pay varies a lot. It depends on when, where, and how much you work. There's a base pay and extra money for overtime. I'd say that a starting reporter makes around $20,000.

"Sales talent is a natural ability — you either have it or you don't."

CRAIG SULLIVAN
TENNIS STORE OWNER
San Francisco, California

WHAT I DO:

I'm the owner and manager of a retail outlet that sells and services tennis equipment. Our specialty is high-end, high-quality racquets and accessories, and in general we're geared to the serious tennis player. We also sell sportswear and tennis shoes.

As the owner of a small business, I stay involved with everything. I keep the store stocked, track the inventory, and even though I have salespeople who sell and string racquets, I do some of this work as well. I also make sure that customers get all the service and information they need. Besides this day-to-day work, I spend a good amount of time keeping track of the industry — communicating with suppliers, making sure they send me what I

Craig restrings a tennis racquet for a customer.

asked for, and making sure it arrives on time.

Another significant part of my time is spent managing our demo program. This program allows a customer to use a trial racquet for three days at a time. It's an effective program because about 60 percent of the people who try racquets buy one. So although the program involves some work — monitoring people, making sure racquets are brought back on time, weeding out those people who aren't serious — it's worth the time I spend on it.

HOW I GOT STARTED:

I've always been active, and interested in athletics and the outdoors. When I was a kid, I played a lot of baseball, rugby, and track. As an adult, I continued with athletics and became a serious tennis player.

I switched jobs fairly often. To make money, I

Craig helps a young player pick the right racquet.

worked in restaurants on and off, but the working environments weren't healthy. The hours were long, and the work was backbreaking. By the time I met the founder of this store, I was ready for a change. I gained his trust, showed him that I knew tennis, and bought myself a partnership in his business contingent on my eventually buying him out. Although this sounds like a risk, I was confident that I could make it work.

HOW I FEEL ABOUT IT:
I like making people happy. I take pride in providing superior service and knowledge of the equipment. It's good to know that when people think of quality and are serious about tennis, I'm the person they think of. In addition, it's fun to sell. I've always been good at disarming people and gaining their trust. So this job allows me to use my natural talents and interests to build a business that I can take pride in, and from which I can earn a living.

The toughest thing about this business is that the profit margins are small, and that it moves in cycles. The tight margins and unpredictability put you under a lot of pressure. You have to be careful not to buy more than you need, and to build a cash cushion for the slow periods. Also, no matter how much capital you have, you've always got to be concerned with bringing in new business. You need to attract customers both for the new goods you sell and the ongoing services you provide.

WHAT YOU SHOULD KNOW: To make a store like mine work, you need sales skills, product knowledge, and accounting skills. I think that sales talent is a natural ability — you either have it or you don't. In any case, I've always felt comfortable selling. As far as product knowledge, that's something you can learn, although it's easier to learn it if you have a real affinity for the sport. Also,

accounting and money management are things that every aspiring business owner should learn.

In this day and age, however, I don't think people should start off on their own. You can't afford the mistakes. You can't expect to wait out two or three years of bad buying decisions and mismanagement and stay in business. So you should start by working for someone else to gain that skill and experience.

This business is a lot of work, but I enjoy doing it. In terms of money, it's a decent living — I'm keeping ahead of the rat race. Although business depends on the year, I generally earn between $30,000 and $60,000.

Craig does everything from inventory to sales.

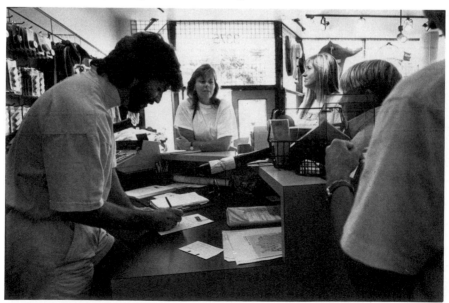

"I keep a book on all the players in the league describing how they hit and run and throw."

BUCK O'NEIL

SCOUT

Kansas City, Missouri

WHAT I DO:
I work for the Kansas City Royals baseball team scouting the other American League teams when they come here to play. By *scout*, I mean that I keep a book on all the other players in the league describing how they hit and run and throw. As the season goes on and I watch the games, I update my book. Eventually, the Royals use this information to help them make trades.

In the off-season, I do a few different things. After the season is over, I go to Florida to watch our instructional league team. It's made up of young players who need more instruction in a particular skill — pitchers who need to work on new pitches, hitters who need to work on their swings. I also spend at least a week in Omaha with the Royals' Triple-A team and another week in Memphis

Buck compares notes on hitting with some of the Royals.

with our Double-A team, making the book on those teams. Then I go to the Royals' spring training camp and report on our own players.

Other scouts also work for the Royals. There's an advance scout who goes on the road and scouts the next opposing team on our schedule. He looks for the strengths and weaknesses of their players so that we can adjust the way we play them. There are also free-agent scouts, who travel around the country looking for young players.

HOW I GOT STARTED:
I've been in baseball since 1934, when I started playing first base for the Miami Giants in the old Negro leagues, as the black leagues were called, in the days before blacks were allowed to play in the white major leagues. In those days, things were a lot different. We barnstormed by bus and train from city to

city. Then, in 1938, I began playing for the Kansas City Monarchs of the Negro American League. Ten years later, I became their player-manager.

While I was in Kansas City, I played with a lot of the great ballplayers — Hilton Smith, Ted Strong, and Satchel Paige. Besides playing in our own league, we also played against great players from the American and National Leagues. Every year, players from the Negro leagues played exhibition games against the great players from the white major leagues. I played on the Satchel Paige All-Stars, and we played against teams like the Dizzy Dean All-Stars and the Bobby Feller All-Stars. These teams had the great stars of their time, men like Babe Ruth and Ralph Kiner.

When I stopped playing in 1955, I went to work for the Chicago Cubs. I became a free-agent scout, going to the local high schools and colleges to look for young talent. I got to scout and sign a lot of great players. One of them, Hall-of-Famer Ernie Banks, was someone I had managed over in Kansas City. I also signed another Hall-of-Famer, Lou Brock. Signing these kinds of players wasn't easy. You had to recognize their talent and also beat

Buck welcomes a new addition to the team.

out all the scouts from the other clubs.

HOW I FEEL ABOUT IT:
I like being in touch with baseball, seeing the players on a regular basis. The job I have now is good because it allows me to stay in Kansas City most of the time, and it keeps me involved with the game.

At this point, I have no problems with the work. I've been in professional baseball for fifty-six years now. I've played a lot of baseball and have seen a lot of other people play it. So I have absolutely no trouble with what I'm doing. I do it. That's it.

WHAT YOU SHOULD KNOW:
At one time, most of the scouts were retired players.

But now it's a little different. A lot of college coaches are going into scouting. There are even some high school coaches who get into it. Of course, I imagine that all these people like baseball and most have wanted to be professional players. But a lot of them never did play any professional ball.

The game and the work of scouting have changed a lot over the years. At one time, when you followed a young player, you might have been the only scout who knew about this player. You could get to know him and his parents. If the player and his parents liked you and your organization, you could sign him. But now, scouting is different. All the young players who want to get into baseball have to go through the draft, a selection system in which teams obtain the exclusive rights to a player. So it doesn't matter how much a scout likes a player, or how much the kid likes the scout and his organization. If the player gets drafted by another team, your team can't have him.

Most scouts make about $20,000, but special assignment scouts like me, who work directly for a team's general manager, can make more, depending on how valuable they are to the team. Some make up to $50,000.

Buck updates his book on other teams' players.

"This job involves a lot more
than being a good golfer."

JOE SHORTO
GOLF PROFESSIONAL

Johnstown, Pennsylvania

WHAT I DO:
I'm the golf professional at Sunnehana Country Club, and I take care of everything that's golf-related at the club. I give lessons, I organize the tournaments, I work with the superintendent and the club manager, and I also run the golf shop. I meet with sales reps, purchase equipment, and sell it to customers. The most important aspect of this job is service — providing for the needs of the golfers at this club, and making sure that their experience is a good one. It begins as soon as a member arrives. I greet the member by name, and the caddie master makes sure his or her clubs are taken from the car.

The tournaments involve the most preparation. After I decide on the type of event, I

Joe is always working to improve his game.

determine the player pairings, entry fee, and prize distribution, and I make up scorecards. Then I decide where to lay out the tee for each hole and the flag on each green, adjusting the difficulty depending on the tournament. In addition, I work with the club manager to coordinate the tournament with any catering for the event. For example, if there's a lunch or dinner, the club manager needs to know when the event will end, so that the meal can begin at a convenient time.

Our active season runs from March until the middle of November depending on the weather. In the off-season, however, there's still a lot to do. At that time, we make plans for the next season, including the tournament schedule. We also have major maintenance to perform on our cart fleet, and we service all of the clubs that we have in storage, about 450 sets. This includes scrubbing the clubs; waxing the shafts, heads, and bags; and covering the bags so that they can be stored safely.

HOW I GOT STARTED:

By the time I was in high school, I was pretty involved with golf and played on the school team. Around that time, I decided to make golf my career. Basically, there are two types of professionals: there's a golf professional, who is a club professional; and there's a professional golfer, who plays on the pro tour. Professional golfers make a lot more money, but I always wanted to go the golf professional route because I enjoyed working with people.

After I got out of college, I got my first job in golf. I was the assistant professional at the Berkeley Hills Golf Course in Johnstown. Then while I was serving in the army reserve, Berkeley Hills offered me the job of head professional when the previous head pro left. I took the position and stayed there for

Joe stops to adjust a student's grip.

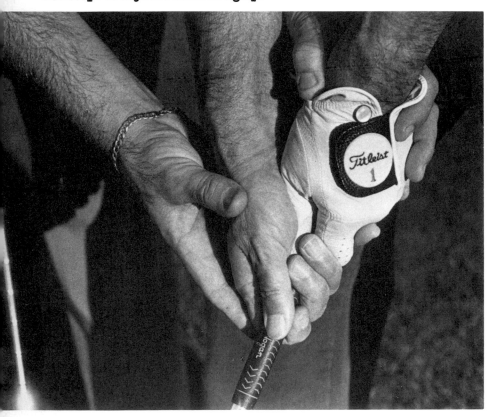

Lessons and customer service are a big part of Joe's job.

a player. It's hard to be good at every one of these functions, so you try to be the best you can and concentrate on those aspects of the job that are your club's main priorities. Sunnehana's priority is service, so I try to make the customers as happy as I can.

WHAT YOU SHOULD KNOW:
If you're interested in becoming a club professional, you can contact the local section of the Professional Golfers Association. They can put you in touch with head pros who are looking for assistants. Once you've found a spot, you serve as a pre-apprentice for six months. If, at that point, you decide that being a golf pro is what you really want to do, the next step is apprenticeship. As an apprentice, you have to serve for thirty-six months under a Class-A professional, pass a playing ability test, and attend and pass two different PGA business schools. These schools are very hard. The failure rate is about 65 percent.

thirteen years. Then, the Sunnehana Country Club offered me their head professional spot. Because it was even more of a challenge, I took it.

HOW I FEEL ABOUT IT:
This job is a big challenge. It involves a lot more than being a good golfer. You have to wear a lot of different hats and be able to communicate effectively with a lot of different people. You're a teacher, an organizer, a merchandiser, and a bookkeeper, as well as

A professional's hours can be very long. The pay depends upon the size and prestige of the club. Someone at a small club might make a salary in the $20,000 range. A professional at a large, prestigious club, however, can make a much higher income.

"If you look in my yearbook where I listed what I wanted to do, it says 'teach physical education.'"

EVA SCOTT

PHYSICAL EDUCATION TEACHER

Baltimore, Maryland

WHAT I DO:
I run the physical education department at a public high school. I'm also the athletic director, and in that capacity I supervise all the inter-scholastic sports. As athletic director, I work with the other coaches — I coach badminton myself — to take care of all of the logistics for games — such as arranging for the transportation, the officials, the scheduling, and so on. Because our program includes quite a few varsity and junior varsity sports, this type of work can take a lot of time.

As chairman of the physical education department, my primary responsibility is making sure the program is adequately supplied. I survey the department's needs and then fill out six or seven different kinds of equipment

Volleyball is only one of the many sports Eva teaches.

requisitions each year. In addition, I drop in on the classes, observe the teachers, write reports, and meet with the staff.

HOW I GOT STARTED:
I have always been interested in sports. I grew up in Baltimore County and played on all the teams at my high school. If you look in my yearbook, at the section where I listed what I wanted to do, it says "teach physical education."

After high school, I went on to college at Morgan State, where I played varsity basketball and volleyball and some other intramural sports. Then I got a master's degree in education and came to Western High School. About ten years after I got here, I was given the title of department head. And a couple of years after that, I was made athletic director. Although these titles didn't really

43

change what I did — I'd always been running the department — they did represent salary increases.

HOW I FEEL ABOUT IT:
The work is very rewarding. I like to see my students progress, and I enjoy their enthusiasm. Some of our students win athletic scholarships to college, and it's very gratifying to see the types of things they do after they've left high school.

If I could change anything about this work, it would have to do with equipment, supplies, and facilities. We're a public high school, and money is tight. It's hard to get everything that we need. There are also major mainte-nance problems that we can't get taken care of as quickly as we'd like. The swimming pool may need work, or the gym floor may need to be redone. But the money just isn't there.

WHAT YOU SHOULD KNOW:
Under the right conditions, I would recommend this work highly. But today I have to qualify that recommendation. People who are interested in this work should know that in many places jobs are being cut. Here in Baltimore, fewer physical education courses are being scheduled — there are almost none in the elementary schools, and very few in the middle schools. It's very difficult for teachers

Eva takes care of the school's athletic equipment.

Eva meets with her physical education staff.

because they don't know, from year to year, whether they will still have a job in the fall. However, if the money is there, and the position is there, it's very fulfilling work.

The pay for physical education teachers in Baltimore starts at $18,000. Administrators can make in the upper $40,000 range. During the school year, which is ten months long, teachers work from 8:00 until at least 3:00, and until 6:00 or 7:00 when they're coaching.

In the summer, I do a little work checking on equipment requisitions. But technically I'm on vacation, so I have time to play sports. I play a lot of tennis, which

is currently my favorite sport. Until about five years ago, I was ranked in the state of Maryland. This past summer, I played singles and doubles badminton in the Maryland state games, and won a silver and a gold medal there.

What I'm doing with tennis and badminton are examples of something we're trying to do with students — develop an interest in what physical education teachers call "lifetime sports." These are sports such as tennis, aerobics, and golf that people can keep playing, and enjoying, as they get older. It's a growing trend, and one that I think will have positive effects for everyone.

"The most rewarding moments are when a team plays beyond its expectations."

BRENDA PAUL

BASKETBALL COACH

Atlanta, Georgia

WHAT I DO:

I coach the women's basketball team at Georgia State University, and I'm responsible for everything related to finding and developing the players. I recruit them, evaluate their talent, coach them on the court, and guide their academic progress. I also take care of the team's scheduling, make travel arrangements, attend conference meetings, and even do a little fund-raising. Because our school is a member of the National Collegiate Athletic Association, another part of my job is keeping up with NCAA rules and regulations.

My work with the players themselves begins in late August when they arrive on campus. This is the first phase of preseason, when we concentrate on weight training, conditioning, and track

Brenda discusses strategy with her players.

work such as sprinting and long-distance running. This continues until October 15, which is the first day that NCAA rules permit organized practice. From then until the season begins in late November, we work on fundamental skills and teamwork.

HOW I GOT STARTED:

I have two older brothers and one older sister, and they all like basketball; so I've always followed the sport — and loved it. I started playing in fourth grade and kept on playing all the way through high school. Around the time I graduated, I decided that I wanted to become a basketball coach.

Once I got into college, I realized that I wanted to coach at the college level. And I felt that the best way to achieve that was to get a master's degree in education. While I did my graduate work, I also taught physical

Brenda gives the team a tough workout every day.

education classes and assisted in the basketball program. That gave other colleges the opportunity to watch me work as an assistant.

One of the schools that liked what they saw was Tennessee Wesleyan University, a small school of about 450 students. They hired me, and I coached there for two years. From there, I moved on to Berry College, which was a national power in women's basketball. After five years there, I went to Mississippi State University, which is an NCAA Division I school. Division I schools are the best in the country, so that was a big step up. After four years there, I came back home to Georgia and took this job at Georgia State, which also has a Division I program.

HOW I FEEL ABOUT IT:
I really love the competition. I also enjoy watching the young people who come into the program reach their athletic and academic potential. It's rewarding to see them mature, achieve success, and decide what they want to do with their lives. In fact, I keep in touch with many of my students. I know what they've done with their lives — how they've used their degrees, how many children they have, and that sort of thing.

As far as the game itself is concerned, the most rewarding moments for me are those when a team plays beyond its expectations. This usually happens in post-season play and in national tournaments. During the season, you might make mistakes as a coach but win anyhow because your team is simply better than the opposition. But in a national tournament, the talent level is pretty much equal, so to win you have to coach a team to play beyond its raw ability.

WHAT YOU SHOULD KNOW:

This isn't just a job. It's a profession, and it demands dedication and sacrifice. First, if you want to become a college coach, it's very important to get a master's degree. You also have to be willing to work as an assistant for little or no money. My first coaching position paid $7200. Beyond that, someone who's thinking of coaching at any level can't be concerned with the number of hours spent on the job. I love the sport, and if that means I have to be in the gym on Saturday and Sunday, that's fine.

When things get very busy during the season, you can put in fourteen to sixteen hours a day. Traveling on the road with your team and scouting other teams takes a lot of time. So does recruitment, when you're out meeting coaches and kids. There is a true off-season — parts of May and August — when coaches take it easy. But don't take this job if you want a nine-to-five life.

The pay at a Division I school is decent, ranging from $30,000 to $45,000 a year, and you can make additional money by giving clinics at summer basketball camps.

Tending to injured players is part of the job.

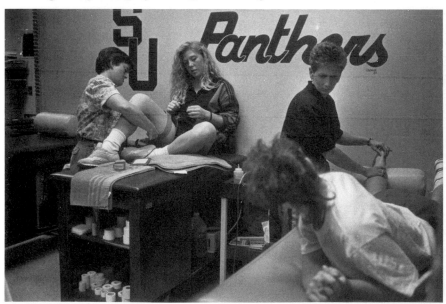

"In this profession, having an easygoing disposition is the key."

EDWARD HILL

SPORTS INFORMATION DIRECTOR

WASHINGTON, D.C.

WHAT I DO:

I work at Howard University. There are seventeen intercollegiate sports played here, and my office keeps statistics and handles publicity for all of them. We print press guides and schedules for all the teams, run all the press operations during the games and matches, and set up interviews with coaches and athletes.

Although the academic year runs only from late August until early June, we operate all year. In the summer, while all the students and professors are on vacation, we prepare for the coming year. During the academic year itself, we go through three seasons of sports — fall, winter, and spring — and there's virtually no breathing room between the seasons.

Edward talks to some football players during a home game.

Because we're responsible for seventeen sports, there's an awful lot for my assistant and me to do. Obviously, we can't be at every home and road game for every sport. But for the major sports, which are men's basketball and football, either my assistant or I work every game because these are the sports that draw the most media and alumni interest — as well as being the revenue-producing sports for the university. When we're there, we make sure that everyone's information is straight — ours, the other school's, and the media's.

For the rest of the sports, we rely on students for much of our information. Each team has either a manager who's on scholarship or a student-athlete, whose responsibility it is to get us game results, as well as to report them to the local media.

HOW I GOT STARTED:

I have always been interested in sports, and I used to be a pretty decent athlete. But I realized a long time ago that I wouldn't be able to play professionally. So I concentrated on another skill that I had — writing.

Writing led me to journalism, which I studied in college. I also assisted the sports information director at my university. Then, after I graduated, I became a sports reporter for the *Winston-Salem Chronicle* and the *Washington Post*. These jobs kept me in contact with the field of sports information, and increased my interest in it.

After about four years of reporting, I took the assistant's job here at Howard, and soon one thing led to another. Within six months, the director took a leave to go to the 1984 Olympics. Although I was still only the assistant in title, I got the opportunity to run the office. When the director returned, he decided to take another job. So I was asked to take his place permanently.

HOW I FEEL ABOUT IT:

The work is very demanding. Besides the sheer volume of information that has to be dealt with, there's the travel. It can really get to you. From September when football starts until March when the basketball season ends, you're moving from city to city, airport to airport, bus to bus. Although it can be exciting, by the end you wonder,

Edward distributes press passes for all the games.

Edward attends as many football games as possible.

"How much longer can I do this?" It's the travel that bothers me more than anything else.

WHAT YOU SHOULD KNOW: People who want to work in this field should get as much relevant experience as possible. While you're in college, you can volunteer as a team manager, learn how to compile statistics, and attend seminars and workshops on journalism. If you're really serious about sports information, one thing that's invaluable is the College Sports Information Directors of America (CoSIDA) convention. All the sports information directors from the United States and Canada attend each year in order to exchange ideas and information. A lot of young people also come to talk to people, get advice, and hand out their résumés.

In this profession, having an easygoing disposition is the key. Because athletics is always in a state of flux, the one thing sports information directors have to be is constant. Whether there's a recruiting problem or a team has won a championship, we can't let ourselves get too low or too high.

The hours and pay vary. There are times when the work is light, and there are times after games when you're busy until midnight. The pay depends on the size of the school and its commitment to the program. Salaries can run anywhere from $12,000 to $45,000, and even more at some of the big football and basketball schools.

"Baseball is like a religion to some people."

TED SPENCER

HALL OF FAME CURATOR

Cooperstown, New York

WHAT I DO:
I design, install, and maintain all the exhibits at the National Baseball Hall of Fame. When you first enter, you're in the Hall of Fame Gallery, which holds the plaques honoring the inductees. On one side of the gallery is the historical wing, which contains exhibits on the World Series, old ball parks, the evolution of the uniform, and such old-time stars as Ty Cobb and Babe Ruth. The other wing focuses more on what's going on now. There we have a records room that shows current and all-time leaders in eighteen different categories, and we also have Baseball Today, a new exhibit about the current teams.

Baseball Today is an example of one of my most important functions as curator — creating up-to-date, graphically interesting ways to present baseball. This exhibit recently replaced an old one that consisted of a series of wall cases, one for each team, with player photos displayed inside. When I planned the new exhibit, I decided to make it into a locker room. We had lockers built for each team. Then we stocked each locker with that team's home and road uniforms, bats, and helmets, as well as baseball cards of the team's current players and a panel that gives a brief team history. As players are traded, we update the exhibit.

Another example of our efforts at graphic innovation is the multi-image theater. This theater, designed to look like a ball park grandstand, shows a thirteen-minute mixed-media tribute to baseball. The theater was built as part of our recent

Ted examines a statue of his namesake, Ted Williams.

Babe Ruth's bat is one of many in the Hall of Fame.

expansion, and I oversaw the putting together of the show.

HOW I GOT STARTED:

I never expected to be doing this. In college, I studied industrial design. Later, I worked for a big corporation doing graphic design and video production, and working on slide presentations. I was very happy and didn't expect to move on. But then I saw this job advertised in a trade journal. The minute I read the ad, I knew it was the opportunity of a lifetime.

The job was perfectly suited to me. My industrial design background qualified me for exhibit design, and the Hall of Fame was looking for someone with just my kind of video and corporate communications experience. Beyond that, baseball was the perfect subject for me because I come from a baseball family — I was even named for Hall-of-Famer Ted Williams — and I love baseball myself. I've been here about eight years now, and I can't imagine a better place to be.

HOW I FEEL ABOUT IT:

As I've said, it's a great combination. I'm working in the

field that I've chosen — design and communication — and I'm working the perfect subject. If you want to communicate effectively, it helps to have a feeling for your subject. And since I love baseball, this job uses my skills to their best advantage.

There really aren't too many problems. I work with good people, and the visitors are mostly great. The few uncomfortable moments usually come from fans. Baseball is like a religion to

Ted works on the design plan for an upcoming exhibit.

some people. They have very strong opinions about it, and their own individual ideas about how it should be represented. Sometimes this leads them to complain about the content of an exhibit. But dealing with that is just part of the job. Over the years, I've developed a thick skin.

WHAT YOU SHOULD KNOW:
Although I'm called a curator, I'm basically still in design — exhibit design. If you're interested in doing this, you need a background in both industrial design and communications. Obviously, you need to know how to make models and mock-ups. But since you're telling a story, you also have to know how to communicate. You need to be able to work with artifacts and images and use them to demonstrate the points you want to make.

Also, the title *curator* means different things in different places. Here, I'm curator for the whole museum, but some museums have a curator for each collection, room, or exhibit space. Naturally, those differences, as well as the differences in museum topic and location, will affect the hours, pay, and duties of the job. If you're one of many curators, you might be making $20,000. Somewhere else, you could be making a lot more than that.

"I learned this business from the ground up."

DIANE OLIN
PRODUCT MANAGER

Chicago, Illinois

WHAT I DO:

I'm a product manager for a sporting goods company, which means that I'm responsible for marketing a particular line of goods. In my case, it's football equipment, particularly helmets. I'm responsible for all of the NFL products that we manufacture: the actual helmets used in NFL games; smaller versions of these helmets for kids; and less expensive models for adults. I'm also responsible for college helmets. I go to the colleges and deal with their representatives.

In addition to product development, however, I'm also involved with the manufacturing end. Here in Chicago, I keep in touch with our director of manufacturing, making sure that all the equipment is being made

Diane examines a souvenir helmet from Super Bowl XXV.

according to specifications and that shipments are going out on time. Finally, I'm responsible for product promotion, so I deal with sales representatives and dealers all across the country and arrange displays at the major sporting goods shows and coaches' conventions. I arrange for booth space, make sure that the samples and displays arrive on time, and arrange for security. I also supervise all the dismantling when we're done.

HOW I GOT STARTED:

I've always been interested in sports. In high school, I played varsity volleyball, soccer, and softball. At college, I played intramural sports and worked part-time in a sporting goods store.

After I graduated, I was promoted to manager of the sporting goods store. My responsibilities included buying, budgeting, and advertising. I stayed there for five years and then moved over to the manufacturing side, where for three years I was a customer service manager. Two years ago, I decided to move on to my present job in marketing.

HOW I FEEL ABOUT IT:

There are a lot of things I like about my work. I like dealing with the stores and showing them how to display our products. I like charting the market and keeping in touch with which teams are popular. I enjoy putting together a good show and seeing that it's running smoothly.

Diane and a colleague prepare for a coaches' convention.

WHAT YOU SHOULD KNOW:

There are a number of different ways to get into this business. I got into it by working in a family-owned retail store and learning the business from the ground up. If you're interested in the manufacturing side, that's a very good way to learn the ropes. It helps you become familiar with all the different manufacturers out there, and gives you some hands-on experience with retailers. It also keys you in to your customers' needs and problems.

Yet this job requires many other skills as well. Besides being good with people, you have to be well organized. And you have to understand

numbers, because there's a lot of forecasting involved. You need to know six months in advance how many San Francisco 49ers helmets people will want to buy. You also need to understand pricing strategies and how and when to adjust them.

The hours are very, very long. During our busy times, when I'm preparing for a conference, I work twelve hours a day, Monday through Saturday. At other times — everything slows down around Christmas, for example — I work only eight or nine hours a day. The pay is good, though. A product manager in this industry can make up to $45,000 a year.

Related Careers

Here are more sports-related careers you may want to explore:

AEROBICS INSTRUCTOR
Aerobics instructors lead group workouts at exercise studios and health clubs.

COLLEGE ATHLETIC DIRECTOR
Athletic directors coordinate and manage all the physical education and intercollegiate sports programs at colleges and universities.

EQUIPMENT DESIGNER
Sports equipment designers design the equipment, such as baseball gloves and tennis racquets, used by athletes.

PERSONAL TRAINER
Personal trainers design customized exercise programs, incuding aerobic training and weight lifting, to suit the individual needs of their clients.

SPORTS ADMINISTRATOR
Sports administrators work for professional leagues and college conferences scheduling games, negotiating contracts, managing officials, and revising and enforcing rules.

SPORTS AGENT
Sports agents represent athletes in contract negotiations with teams, professional leagues, and product sponsors.

SPORTS CAMP DIRECTOR
Sports camp directors manage camps that focus on improving skills in a particular sport such as tennis, football, or gymnastics.

SPORTS DOCTOR
Sports doctors specialize in treating athletes who suffer sports-related injuries such as injuries to bones, joints, and muscles.

SPORTS PHOTOGRAPHER
Sports photographers take pictures of athletes and sporting events for newspapers and magazines.

SPORTS PROMOTER
Sports promoters arrange sporting events such as boxing matches, car races, and exhibition games.

SPORTS PSYCHOLOGIST
Sports psychologists help athletes cope with the pressures of competition.

STATISTICIAN
Statisticians keep official records of team performance such as players' batting averages in baseball or shooting percentages in basketball.

Organizations

Contact these organizations for information about the following careers:

PHYSICAL EDUCATION TEACHER
American Alliance for Health, Physical Education, Recreation, and Dance
1900 Association Drive, Reston, VA 22091

SPORTS LAWYER
American Bar Association
1800 M Street, N.W., Suite 200, Washington, DC 20036

FOOTBALL COACH
American Football Coaches Association
7758 Wallace Road, Orlando, FL 32819

SPORTSWRITER
Football Writers Association of America
Box 1022, Edmund, OK 73034

BASKETBALL OFFICIAL
International Association of Approved Basketball Officials
P.O. Box 661, West Hartford, CT 06107

BASKETBALL COACH
National Association of Basketball Coaches of the United States
18 Orchard Avenue, Branford, CT 06405

SPORTS ANNOUNCER
National Association of Broadcasters
1771 N Street, N.W., Washington, DC 20036

SCOUT, BASEBALL EXECUTIVE
National Baseball Congress
Box 1420, Wichita, KS 67201

HOCKEY OFFICIAL
National Hockey League
650 Fifth Avenue, New York, NY 10019

GOLF PROFESSIONAL
Professional Golfers Association of America
P.O. Box 12458, Palm Beach Gardens, FL 33410

PRO TENNIS PLAYER
United States Professional Tennis Association
1620 Gulf of Mexico Drive, Longboat Key, FL 33548

TENNIS OFFICIAL
United States Tennis Association
1212 Avenue of the Americas, New York, NY 10036

Books

CAREERS AND OPPORTUNITIES IN SPORTS
By Stan Isaacs. New York: Dutton, 1964.

CAREERS IN SPORTS
By Bob and Marquita McGonagle. New York: Lothrop, Lee & Shepard, 1975.

CAREERS IN SPORTS
By Jack Clary. Chicago: Contemporary Books, 1982.

CAREERS IN THE SPORTS INDUSTRY
By Barbara Fenten. New York: Franklin Watts, 1977.

DEVELOPING A CAREER IN SPORT
By Greg J. Cylkowski. Ithaca, N.Y.: Mouvement Publications, 1988.

EXPLORING APPRENTICESHIP CAREERS
By Charlotte Lobb. New York: Rosen Publishing, 1985.

MODERN SPORTSWRITING
By Louis I. Gelfand and Harry E. Heath. Ames: Iowa University Press, 1969.

OFFBEAT CAREERS: THE DIRECTORY OF UNUSUAL WORK
By Al Sacharov. Berkeley, Cal.: Ten Speed Press, 1988.

OPPORTUNITIES IN FITNESS CAREERS
By Jean Rosenbaum, M.D., and Mary Prine, R.N. Lincolnwood, Ill.: VGM, 1986.

OPPORTUNITIES IN MARKETING CAREERS
By Margery Steinberg. Lincolnwood, Ill.: VGM, 1988.

OPPORTUNITIES IN SPORTS AND ATHLETICS
By William Ray Heitzmann. Lincolnwood, Ill.: VGM, 1985.

SPORTS REPORTING
By Bruce Garrison. Ames: Iowa State University Press, 1985.

THE STUDENT JOURNALIST AND SPORTS REPORTING
By Harry Stapler. New York: Richards Rosen, 1964.

TEACHING INDIVIDUAL AND TEAM SPORTS
By Raymond Talmadge De Witt. Englewood Cliffs, N.J.: Prentice-Hall, 1972.

Glossary Index